MATH MASTERS  ANALYZE THIS!

All About AREA

Claire Piddock

Rourke
Educational Media

rourkeeducationalmedia.com

Scan for Related Titles and
Teacher Resources

Before Reading:

Building Academic Vocabulary and Background Knowledge

Before reading a book, it is important to tap into what your child or students already know about the topic. This will help them develop their vocabulary, increase their reading comprehension, and make connections across the curriculum.

1. *Look at the cover of the book. What will this book be about?*
2. *What do you already know about the topic?*
3. *Let's study the Table of Contents. What will you learn about in the book's chapters?*
4. *What would you like to learn about this topic? Do you think you might learn about it from this book? Why or why not?*
5. *Use a reading journal to write about your knowledge of this topic. Record what you already know about the topic and what you hope to learn about the topic.*
6. *Read the book.*
7. *In your reading journal, record what you learned about the topic and your response to the book.*
8. *After reading the book complete the activities below.*

Content Area Vocabulary
Read the list. What do these words mean?

addend
area
compound
formula
parallel
product
solid
sum
surface area
unit square

After Reading:

Comprehension and Extension Activity

After reading the book, work on the following questions with your child or students in order to chec their level of reading comprehension and content mastery.

1. *How can you find the area of a parallelogram?* (Summarize)
2. *How can you break apart and put together the area of rectangles?* (Infer)
3. *What is a formula?* (Asking questions)
4. *Name an easy way to find the area of a shape you read about in the book.* (Text to self connectic
5. *What is area and how can you measure it?* (Asking questions)

Extension Activity

Practice all the concepts in this book to master all about area!

Table of Contents

Measuring Up!

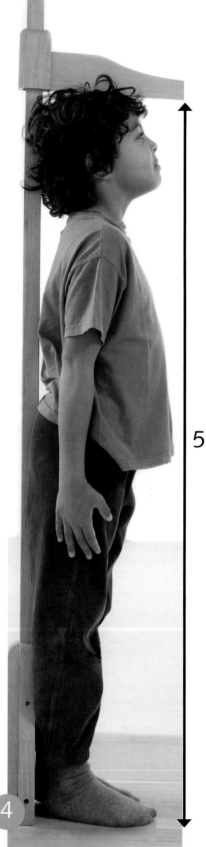

51 inches

What do you measure?

You can measure length, such as how many inches tall you are...or how many inches long your bike is.

45 inches

You can also measure **area**. Area is the space that a flat shape or figure covers.

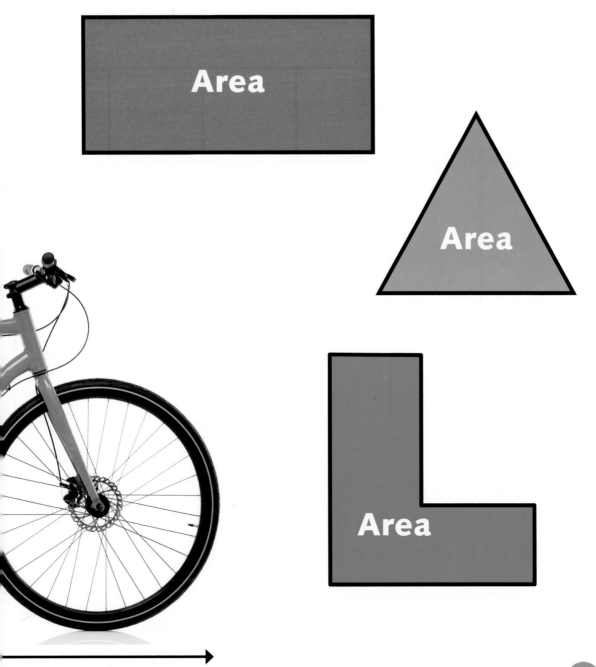

Counting Unit Squares

Measure the area of a shape by counting the number of unit squares. Each box below is a **unit square**.

1	2	3	4	5	6
7	8	9	10	11	12
13	14	15	16	17	18
19	20	21	22	23	24

The shape is covered by 24 unit squares.

The area is 24 square units.

Always label the answer in square units.

Measure the area of this checkerboard by counting all the square units.

Answer:
64 square units

Unit squares can be different sizes.
This unit square measures
1 square centimeter.
This means that each of its sides is 1 centimeter long.

This unit square measures
1 square inch. This means
that each of its sides is
1 inch long.

Area Shortcut: Multiply!

You can count the square units to find the area of this rectangle.

width							
1	2	3	4	5	6	7
8	9	10	11	12	13	14

length

Here is an easier way to find the area. Multiply length times width. The shape is 7 units long and 2 units wide.

Area = length times width

Area = 7 units x 2 units = 14 square units

You don't even need to see the unit squares. Just multiply the lengths of the sides of a rectangle. The **product** is the area.

- Uh oh! What if you play ball and break a window? What is the area of the glass that needs to be replaced?

Area Formulas: Rectangles

A **formula** is a scientific or mathematical rule that is written with numbers and symbols. A formula shows letters and math operations such as +, −, x, and ÷. Replace the letters with the numbers you are given. Then carry out the operations.

$$A = l \times w \text{ and } A = s \times s$$

Area of a Rectangle

$A = l \times w$

$A = 11$ yards $\times$ 3 yards

$A = 33$ square yards

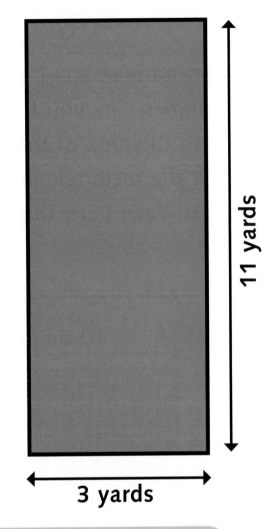

11 yards

3 yards

In a square, the length and width are the same, because each of its sides measures the same. So the formula for the area of a square is $A = s \times s$, where we use s to represent how much each of its sides measures.

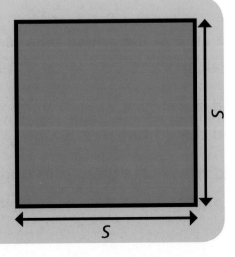

s

s

Combining Areas

You can break apart and put together the area of rectangles. Say you forgot how to multiply 9 x 18 to find the area of the blue rectangle.
Break the rectangle into two parts, find the area of each part, then add the areas together.

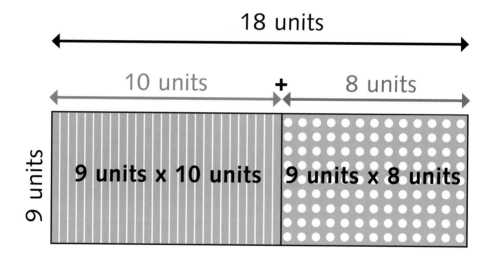

The area of the whole blue rectangle is *l* x *w* or 9 units x 18 units.
Break apart 18 units into 10 units + 8 units to make two rectangles.

Find the striped area: 9 units x 10 units = 90 square units
Find the dotted area: 9 units x 8 units = 72 square units

Add the areas together to find the area of the blue rectangle.
90 square units + 72 square units = 162 square units

The computation shows the Distributive Property: It says multiplying a **sum** by a number is the same as multiplying each **addend** by the number and then adding the products.

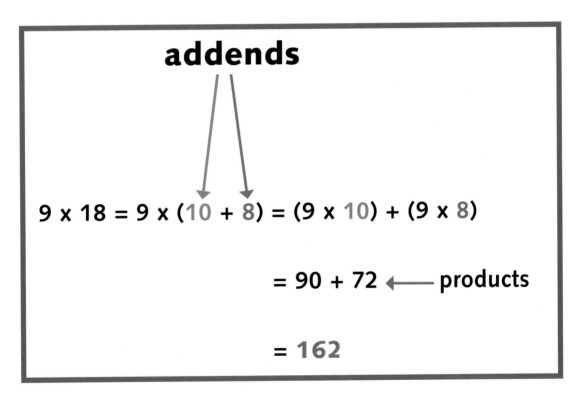

addends

$9 \times 18 = 9 \times (10 + 8) = (9 \times 10) + (9 \times 8)$

$= 90 + 72 \longleftarrow$ products

$= 162$

Compound Figures

Hmmm. This shape is not a rectangle, but you can still find its area. This is a **compound** figure made up of two or more figures put together.

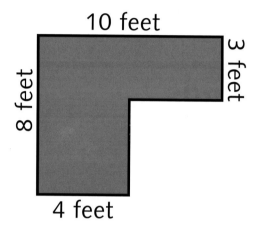

Break the figure apart into two smaller rectangles.

Here is one way.

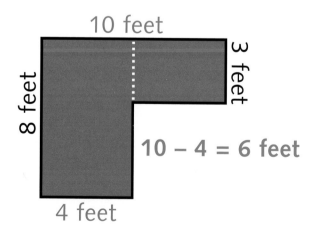

Area of left rectangle: $l \times w$

8 feet x 4 feet = 32 square feet

Area of right rectangle: $l \times w$

6 feet x 3 feet = 18 square feet

Total Area = 32 square feet + 18 square feet

= 50 square feet

Here is another way.

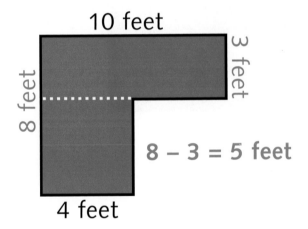

10 feet

8 feet

3 feet

8 – 3 = 5 feet

4 feet

Area of top rectangle: $l \times w$

10 feet x 3 feet = 30 square feet

Area of bottom rectangle: $l \times w$

4 feet x 5 feet = 20 square feet

Total Area = 30 square feet + 20 square feet

= 50 square feet

Buddies: Area and Perimeter

18 feet

15 feet

Perimeter is the distance around a figure. You find the perimeter by adding the length of all of its sides.

You can have figures with the same area and different perimeters. You can have figures with the same perimeter and different areas.

Area = l x w

= 18 inches x 15 inches

= 270 square inches

Perimeter = l + w + l + w

= 18 inches + 15 inches

+ 18 inches + 15 inches

= 66 inches

Explore area and perimeter. What is the same?
What is different in each pair of shapes?

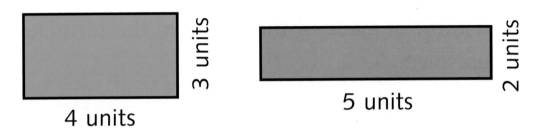

Perimeters are the same. Areas are different.

Green shape: **P** = 14 units; **A** = 12 square units
Orange shape: **P** = 14 units; **A** = 10 square units

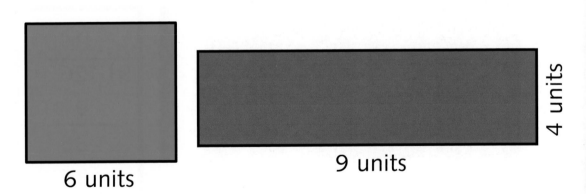

Areas are the same. Perimeters are different.

Blue shape: **A** = 36 square units; **P** = 24 units
Red shape: **A** = 36 square units; **P** = 26 units

What's Missing?

Sometimes you know the area and just one side of a shape. To find what's missing, put the numbers you know in place of the letters in the formula. Then solve.

This rug's a rectangle with an area of 126 square feet. Its width measures 9 feet. What is the length of the rug?

9 feet

?

$$A = l \times w$$

126 square feet = l feet x 9 feet

To find l, divide 126 square feet by 9 feet.

$$
\begin{array}{r}
\,\,14 \\
9\overline{)\,126} \\
-\,9 \\
\hline
36 \\
-\,36 \\
\hline
0 \\
\end{array}
$$

The length of the rug is 14 feet.

Watch out! Use area formulas to solve this tricky problem.

- Max and her brother built a square work table with sides 10 feet long. They want to build another work table with the same area and a length of 20 feet. What will be the width of their new work table?

Answer:
5 feet

Area of Other Figures

How can you find the area of a parallelogram?
A parallelogram is a 4-sided figure with opposite
sides that are **parallel** and equal in length.

A rectangle is a parallelogram with square corners.

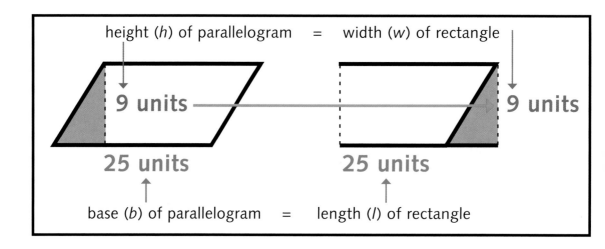

Slide a piece of the parallelogram to the other end.
The parallelogram becomes a rectangle with the
same area.

Instead of length (*l*) times width (*w*),
we use base (*b*) x height (*h*)

Area of parallelogram: $A = b \times h$

The area of both is **9 units** x **25 units** or **225 square units**.

- Sam's sign has a base that is 11 inches long. The sign is 30 inches tall. What is the area of Sam's sign?

30 inches

11 inches

How can you find the area of a triangle?

If you draw a line between opposite corners, you see a triangle is half of a parallelogram. The triangle has the same base and the same height as the parallelogram.

Area of a triangle: $A = \frac{1}{2} \times b \times h$

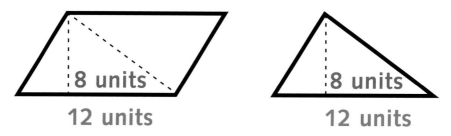

The area of the parallelogram is the base times the height or **8 units** x **12 units** = **72 square units**.
The area of the triangle is half that or 36 square units.

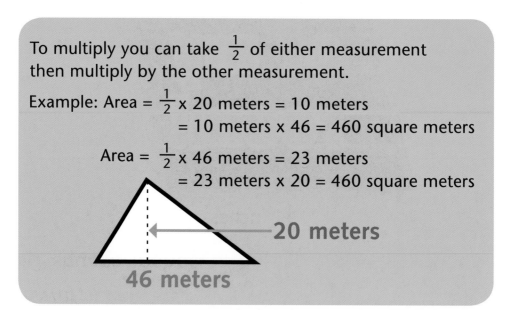

To multiply you can take $\frac{1}{2}$ of either measurement then multiply by the other measurement.

Example: Area = $\frac{1}{2}$ x 20 meters = 10 meters
= 10 meters x 46 = 460 square meters

Area = $\frac{1}{2}$ x 46 meters = 23 meters
= 23 meters x 20 = 460 square meters

20 meters

46 meters

- Sofia's sandwich bread is a triangle. What is the area of the bread in this half sandwich?

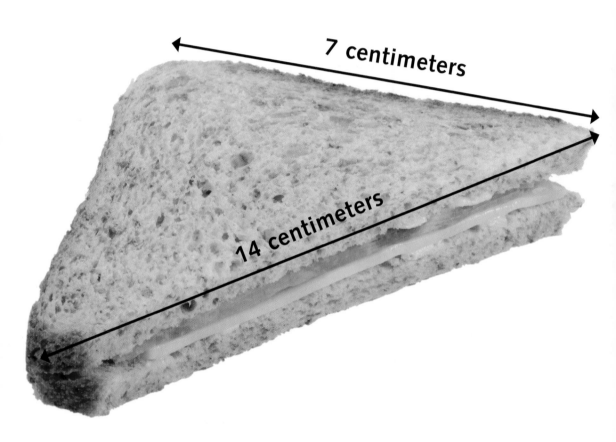

7 centimeters

14 centimeters

Surface Area

Many **solid** figures are simply folded up flat pieces.

Here are 6 connected squares that are all the same size. Each side is 2 inches long.

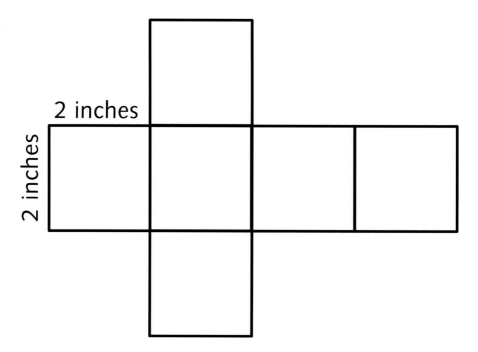

The area of one square is

    2 inches x 2 inches = 4 square inches

The whole shape has 6 of those small squares.

The area of the whole shape is

    6 x 4 square inches = 24 square inches

If you fold up this flat shape, you make a cube.
The **surface area** of the cube is 24 square inches.

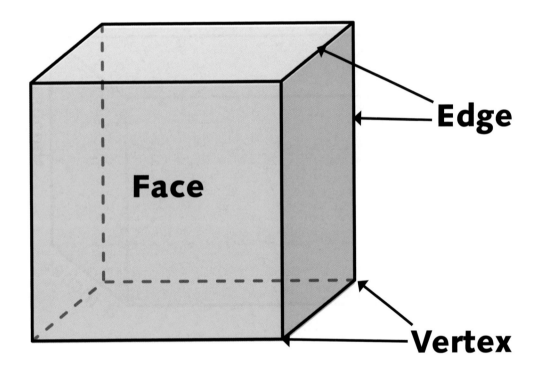

Each flat surface of a solid figure is called a face.
Each corner is a vertex.
The side where faces meet are edges.
The surface area is the sum of the areas of all the
faces of a figure.

Here is a block made up of different rectangles.

You need to paint all surfaces of the block.

How do you find the area that the paint must cover?

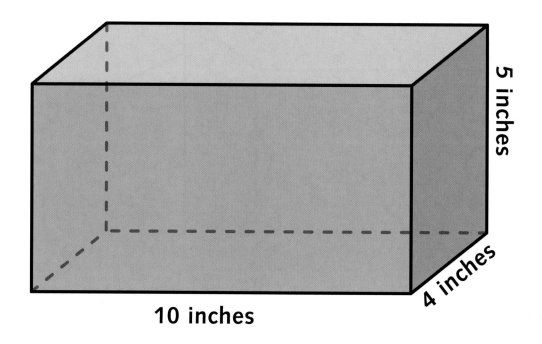

5 inches

4 inches

10 inches

This is a rectangular prism. It has six faces that are all rectangles. Opposite faces are the same size and shape.

Think of the unfolded rectangular prism to find the surface area.

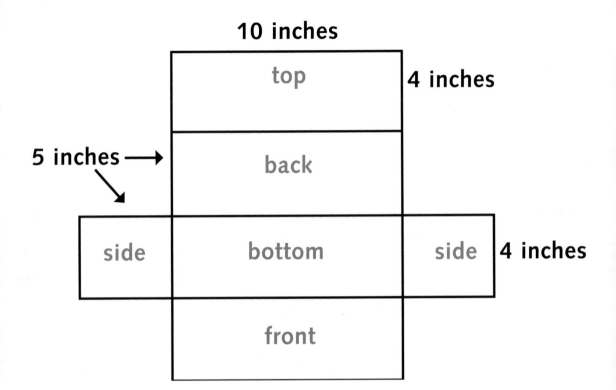

Top and bottom: Areas = 2 x (4 inches x 10 inches)
= 2 x 40 square inches = 80 square inches

Front and back: Areas = 2 x (5 inches x 10 inches)
= 2 x 50 square inches = 100 square inches

Sides: Areas = 2 x (4 inches x 5 inches)
= 2 x 20 square inches = 40 square inches

Surface area: = 80 square inches
100 square inches
+ 40 square inches
_____
220 square inches

Here is a wooden block made up of triangles
and rectangles. If you paint the block, what
area will the paint cover?

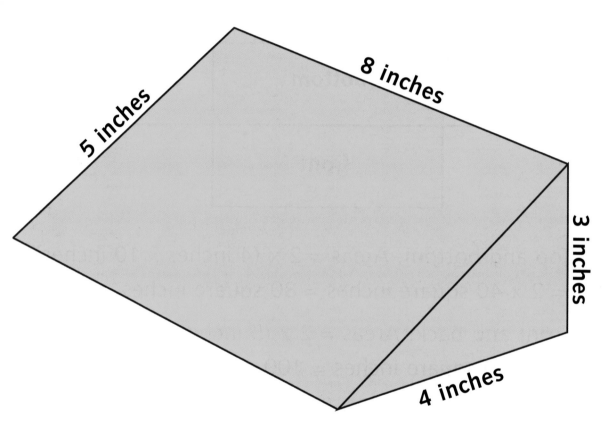

This is a triangular prism. Two opposite faces are equal
triangles. Three faces are rectangles with a width equal to the
length of one side of the triangle.

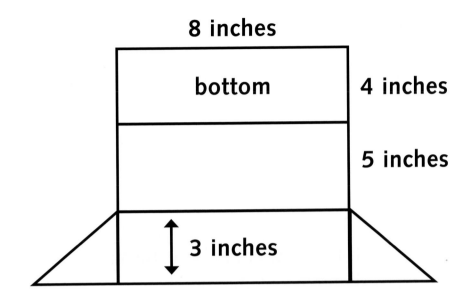

8 inches

bottom

4 inches

5 inches

3 inches

Area of rectangles:

3 inches x 8 inches = 24 square inches

5 inches x 8 inches = 40 square inches

4 inches x 8 inches = 32 square inches

Area of triangles: $2 \times \frac{1}{2} \times (4 \text{ inches} \times 3 \text{ inches})$

$= 2 \times \frac{1}{2} \times 12$ square inches

$= 2 \times 6$ square inches $= 12$ square inches

Surface area =   24 square inches

40 square inches

32 square inches

+ 12 square inches

108 square inches

Glossary

addend (AD-end): any number that is added to another number to form a sum

area (AIR-ee-uh): the amount of surface within a given boundary, measured in square units

compound (KAHM-pound): something formed by combining two or more parts

formula (FOR-myuh-luh): a scientific or mathematical rule that is written with numbers and symbols

parallel (PAR-uh-lel): staying the same distance from each other and never crossing or meeting

product (PRAH-duhkt): the number you get when you multiply two or more numbers

solid (SAH-lid): an object that has length, width, and height

sum (suhm): the number you get from adding two or more numbers together

surface area (SUR-fis AIR-ee-uh): the sum of the areas of all the faces, or surfaces, of a solid figure

unit square (YOO-nit skwair): a square that measures one unit on each side, such as one inch, one meter, or one foot, that can be used to measure area

Index

Websites to Visit

www.ixl.com/math/grade-4/area-of-squares-and-rectangles

www.commoncoresheets.com/Area.php

www.mathworksheets4kids.com/area.html

About The Author

Claire Piddock lives by a pond in the woods of Maine with her husband and big dog, Otto. She loves painting landscapes, doing puzzles, and reading mysteries. She sees math as a fun puzzle and enjoys taking the mystery out of math as she has done for many years as a teacher and writer.

Meet The Author!
www.meetREMauthors.com

© 2017 Rourke Educational Media

www.rourkeeducationalmedia.com

PHOTO CREDITS: Cover diagrams © EtiAmmos, lightbulb "brain" © Positive Vectors; page 4 boy © JPC-PROD, bike © Vladyslav Starozhylov, page 7 checkerboard © Sergej Razvodovskij, page 9 © Andrea Crisante, page 10 © Wolfgang Zwanzger, page 16 frame © denispro, dog © The Dog Photographer, page 18 © Petinov Sergey Mihilovich, page 19 © Phovoir; page 23 © Phovoir; pages 25, 26 © aekikuis; page 28 © Fouad A. Saad; All images from Shutterstock.com except page 9 from Dreamstime.com

Edited by: Keli Sipperley

Cover and Interior design by: Nicola Stratford   www.nicolastratford.com

Library of Congress PCN Data

All About Area / Claire Piddock
(Math Masters: Analyze This!)
ISBN 978-1-68191-731-3 (hard cover)
ISBN 978-1-68191-832-7 (soft cover)
ISBN 978-1-68191-925-6 (e-Book)
Library of Congress Control Number: 2016932654

Rourke Educational Media
Printed in the United States of America, North Mankato, Minnesota

Also Available as: